A LIBERIAN FAMILY

A LIBERIAN FAMILY

By Stephen Chicoine

Lerner Publications Company • Minneapolis

The interviews for this book were conducted in late 1995 and in 1996.

This book is available in two editions:
Library binding by Lerner Publications Company
Soft cover by First Avenue Editions
241 First Avenue North
Minneapolis, MN 55401
ISBN: 0–8225–3411–8 (lib. bdg.)
ISBN: 0–8225–9758–6 (pbk.)

A pronunciation guide can be found on page 62

LIBRARY OF CONGRESS CATALOGING-IN-PUBLICATION DATA

Chicoine, Stephen.
    A Liberian family / by Stephen Chicoine.
      p. cm. — (Journey between two worlds)
    Includes index.
    Summary: Describes the events that led to civil war in the West African republic of Liberia and the efforts of one Liberian family to emigrate to the United States and rebuild their lives in Houston, Texas.
    ISBN 0–8225–3411–8 (lib. bdg. : alk. paper)
1. Liberian American families—Texas—Houston—Juvenile literature.
2. Liberian Americans—Texas—Houston—Juvenile literature. 3. Refugees, Political—Texas—Houston—Juvenile literature. 4. Refugees, Political—Liberia—Juvenile literature. 5. Houston (Tex.)—Social life and customs—Juvenile literature. [1. Liberian Americans. 2. Refugees. 3. Liberia—History—Civil War, 1989–] I. Title. II. Series.
F394.H89L53 1997
976.4'141106—dc20   96–16739

Manufactured in the United States of America
1 2 3 4 5 6 – SP – 02 01 00 99 98 97

AUTHOR'S NOTE

I would like to thank the entire Miller family for their willingness to share their very personal story with me and for their easy acceptance of me into their lives. My friendship with Francis Miller and his family has extended beyond the experience of creating this book. I also want to thank the Millers for teaching me new dimensions of perseverance and faith in God.

My friend the Reverend Dr. Charles Greene was most helpful in introducing me to the Miller family. Their ready acceptance of me is indicative of Dr. Greene's close relationship with his congregation at Gethsemane United Methodist Church in Houston, Texas, and of the truly Christian way in which its community functions. Shadrach Walker also kindly offered advice and comments on his native Liberia.

Finally, my wife, Mary Ann, was understanding, patient, and supportive throughout the many hours I spent getting to know the Millers and writing their story.

This book is dedicated to Brent Ashabranner, writer, humanitarian, and mentor, and a man who retains a special place in his heart for West Africa.

Refugees (above) *from Liberia flee their homeland, where war has become a way of life. International relief agencies provide food* (facing page) *to many of the refugees.*

SERIES INTRODUCTION

 What they have left behind is sometimes a living nightmare of war and hunger that most Americans can hardly begin to imagine. As refugees set out to start a new life in another country, they are torn by many feelings. They may wish they didn't have to leave their homeland. They may fear giving up the only life they have ever known. Many may also feel excitement and hope as they struggle to build a better life in a new country.

People who move from one place to another are called migrants. Two types of migrants are immigrants and refugees. Immigrants choose to leave their homelands, usually to improve their standards of living. They may be leaving behind poverty, famine (hunger), or a failing economy. They may be pursuing a better job or reuniting with family members.

Rebel armies have been fighting since the late 1980s for control of Liberia. This soldier is part of the United Liberation Movement of Liberia for Democracy (ULIMO), one of the rebel groups.

Refugees, on the other hand, often have no choice but to flee their homeland to protect their own personal safety. How could anyone be in so much danger? The government of his or her country is either unable or unwilling to protect its citizens from persecution, or cruel treatment. In many cases, the government is actually the cause of the persecution. Government leaders or another group within the country may be persecuting anyone of a certain race, religion, or ethnic background. Or they may persecute those who belong to a particular social group or who hold political opinions that are not accepted by the government.

From the 1950s through the mid-1970s, the number of refugees worldwide held steady at between 1.5 and 2.5 million. The number began to rise sharply in 1976. By the mid-1990s, it approached 20 million. These figures do not include people who are fleeing disasters such as famine (estimated to be at least 10 million). Nor do they include those who are forced to leave their homes but stay within their own countries (about 27 million).

As this rise in refugees and other migrants continues, countries that have long welcomed newcomers are beginning to close their doors. Some U.S. citizens question whether the United States should accept refugees when it cannot even meet the needs of all its own people. On the other hand, experts point out

A Liberian family makes do in a refugee camp.

that the number of refugees is small—less than 20 percent of all migrants worldwide—so refugees really don't have a very big impact on the nation. Still others suggest that the tide of refugees could be slowed through greater efforts to address the problems that force people to flee. There are no easy answers in this ongoing debate.

This book is one in a series called *Journey Between Two Worlds*, which looks at the lives of refugee families—their difficulties and triumphs. Each book describes the journey of a family from their homeland to the United States and how they adjust to a new life in America while still preserving traditions from their homeland. The series makes no attempt to join the debate about refugees. Instead, *Journey Between Two Worlds* hopes to give readers a better understanding of the daily struggles and joys of a refugee family.

(Left to right) *Kau, Deazee, Augustus, and Thomas Miller hang out on the porch of the family's apartment in Houston, Texas.*

"Did you hear they are killing again?" Maryetta King shakes her head in disbelief. She has just heard the latest news of the civil war in her homeland of Liberia, a country in West Africa. Maryetta shares a three-bedroom apartment in Houston, Texas, with her daughter Pearl Miller, her daughter's husband, Francis Miller, their five children—Augustus (17), Nya (16), Thomas (13), Kau (12), and Deazee (10)—and Francis's brother Thomas.

In 1990 the Miller family fled Liberia to escape the brutal civil war that was destroying their country. Kau was only seven years old when she left the family's home in Monrovia, Liberia's capital city. Kau recalls how her neighborhood became a war zone. "We could hear the fighting. Sometimes it was near us. We could hear gunshots everywhere."

Food was hard to find in the war-torn city. So Francis left Monrovia to search for food. While he was gone, the war worsened, and Kau and her brothers fled the city with their mother, Pearl. Once outside of Monrovia, Pearl and the children continued eastward across Liberia toward the safety of Côte d'Ivoire (Ivory Coast), a neighboring country.

Kau remembers the dangerous journey. She and her family walked all day and found shelter wherever they could at night. Kau says, "It [took] a long time. Everywhere we walked, soldiers would stop us."

The soldiers seized what few possessions people were carrying. The refugees didn't dare protest because the soldiers shot and killed whomever they chose. Kau recalls, "At nighttime, when we were trying to sleep, they would be firing their guns. There would always be shooting."

Kau (left) *was afraid when her father, Francis* (right), *left Monrovia to find food for the family.*

Monrovia, Liberia, had a population of about 425,000 before civil war destroyed the city.

The Republic of Liberia, a country about the size of the state of Ohio, is located on the western coast of Africa. Because Liberia lies close to the equator, the country's climate is hot and humid. Temperatures can rise as high as 120° F (49° C). The republic shares borders with Sierra Leone on the northwest, Guinea on the north, and Côte d'Ivoire on the east. The Atlantic Ocean forms Liberia's western and southern coasts.

Liberia's largest cities are along the coast. Farther inland the landscape is hilly and covered with dense, tropical rain forests. Several mountain ranges, including the Wologizi and the Nimba Mountains, rise in Liberia's interior. Rivers generally flow southward across the land on their way to the Atlantic Ocean.

Monrovia, where the Millers lived before fleeing civil war, lies along the northwestern section of Liberia's coast.

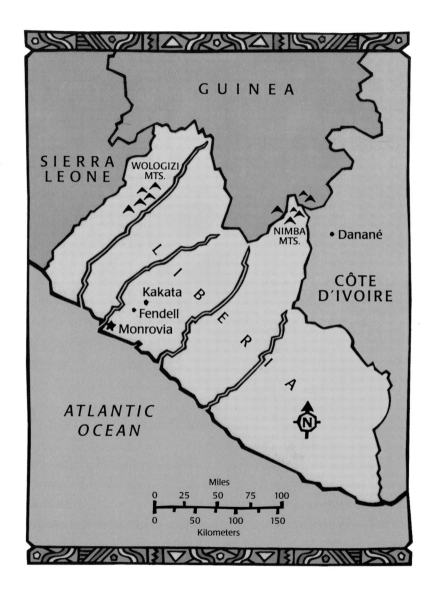

GUINEA

SIERRA LEONE

WOLOGIZI MTS.

NIMBA MTS.

• Danané

CÔTE D'IVOIRE

L I B E R I A

• Kakata
• Fendell
★ Monrovia

ATLANTIC OCEAN

N

Miles
0   25   50   75   100

0   50   100   150
Kilometers

English is Liberia's official language. But the republic has 16 major ethnic groups, each of which speaks its own languages. Christianity and Islam are Liberia's main religions. Many Liberians also practice the traditional beliefs of their ethnic group.

When the civil war began in late 1989, Liberia was home to about 2.8 million people. Since then almost half of Liberia's population have lost their homes. Close to 200,000 people have been killed, and about 750,000 people have fled the country. Some of these refugees went to the United States, with which Liberia has a long history.

The Republic of Liberia had its beginnings as a U.S. colony (overseas settlement) in the early 1800s. At that time, more than 700,000 black slaves lived in the United States. Most of them were forced to work on large plantations (farms) in the southern part of the country. In some parts of the South, slaves made up more than half the population.

Most black slaves had family roots in West Africa. Starting in the 1500s, European slave traders took Africans by force from their homelands in this vast region. The traders transported the Africans by ship across the Atlantic Ocean to the Americas, where the slaves were sold at slave auctions. Through the slave trade, which lasted about 300 years, millions of black slaves were brought to the southern United States.

A 13-year-old rebel fighter, one of many boy soldiers fighting in Liberia, carries an AK-47 assault rifle strapped around his neck as he rides his bicycle through the streets of Monrovia.

Black workers sweep a yard in Belton, South Carolina. Even after slavery was outlawed, blacks in the United States suffered discrimination that kept them from getting an education or securing a good job.

Not everyone in the United States was in favor of slavery. By 1808 bringing slaves to the United States was illegal. Over time some black slaves gained their freedom. A few slave owners, for example, set slaves free. Other slaves bought their own freedom. By 1820 about 200,000 free blacks were living in the United States.

Many slaveholders felt they couldn't make a living without cheap slave labor. These slaveholders worried that free blacks in the United States would lead revolts to end slavery. For this reason, slave owners and other people who supported slavery encouraged free black people to return to West Africa. Some supporters of slavery wanted all free blacks to be forced to return to Africa.

In 1816 the American Colonization Society (ACS) was formed to transport free blacks to West Africa. Many of the founders of the ACS were slaveholders. Others were ministers who hoped that free blacks would teach Christianity to native peoples in Africa. Some leaders of the ACS were against slavery. They thought the society's plan would give free blacks a chance to start a new life in a place where they would not suffer from discrimination and prejudice as they did in the United States.

Samuel Cornish (left) *and John Russwurm* (right) *published* Freedom's Journal, *the first U.S. newspaper run by blacks. These and other prominent blacks opposed the viewpoints and the goals of the American Colonization Society, arguing that the organization aimed to force free blacks out of the United States to strengthen slavery in the South.*

U.S. President James Monroe assisted the ACS in transporting free blacks to West Africa. When Liberia became a nation, Monrovia—named after the president—was made its capital.

Some free blacks volunteered enthusiastically to return to their ancestral homes in West Africa. But most free blacks felt that the United States was their rightful home. As a result, only about 12,000 free blacks journeyed across the Atlantic Ocean to West Africa.

With the support of the U.S. government, including President James Monroe, the first group of black colonists (settlers) left the United States in 1820 for what is now Liberia. When the colonists arrived, they ran into problems. Bad weather and lack of supplies made farming difficult. Many people fell ill and died from malaria and other tropical diseases. Local African peoples viewed the newcomers as invaders. Armed conflict broke out between the two groups in 1822. Even after a peace treaty (agreement) was signed, local African peoples and the colonists did not get along well.

The Miller children can trace their ancestry to the ACS settlers. Maryetta's great-great-grandmother was among the early colonists. Maryetta remembers her mother telling her that this woman was "a strong Christian woman."

The settlements that the colonists established along the coast of West Africa became known as Liberia. This name comes from the Latin word *liber,* which means "free." ACS agents ruled Liberia until it became an independent republic in 1847. Monrovia, the original colonist settlement, became Liberia's capital city.

A page from an 1868 U.S. newspaper describes the growth of the Republic of Liberia during its first 20 years. Clockwise from bottom: Monrovia; the first president of Liberia, J. J. Roberts; the presidential mansion in Monrovia; and the U.S. consul general, John Seys.

The Liberian flag, which was modeled after the U.S. flag, has eleven stripes— one for each person who signed the Liberian Declaration of Independence.

The United States maintained its ties to Liberia even after the country gained independence. In the 1920s, the Firestone Tire and Rubber Company of Akron, Ohio, rented land in Liberia for huge rubber plantations. Many Liberians welcomed the company, which provided jobs for unemployed Liberians, built roads and schools, and lent the republic money to pay off its immediate debts. Producing rubber for the United States and other countries has been a major part of Liberia's economy ever since.

The descendants of the original ACS settlers who did not intermarry with Liberia's native peoples came to be known in Liberia as Americo-Liberians. This group makes up only a small part of Liberia's population. Most people belong to one of Liberia's 16 native ethnic groups. But Americo-Liberians have ruled the republic for most of its history.

Over time Monrovia and the smaller communities along Liberia's coast developed into modern cities. But traditional farming villages in Liberia's interior did not. Schools and hospitals were not available in many of these areas. Between 1960 and 1990, villagers from the interior began heading to the cities on the coast to look for jobs. Others, like Francis Miller, who was of the Mano tribe, went to Monrovia for education. Over a 30-year period, the capital city's population mushroomed from 80,000 to nearly half a million people.

A worker on a Firestone plantation in Liberia taps a rubber tree to harvest latex, the thick, milky liquid from which rubber can be made.

With good schooling, Francis was able to find a desirable job in Monrovia as a radio technician for the Voice of America—an international U.S.-government radio station. But many of Liberia's native peoples lacked job skills and education. As a result, they couldn't find work in the cities, where many people lived in poverty. In addition, most good jobs and other opportunities went to Americo-Liberians, who were the country's wealthiest and most powerful citizens. These unequal conditions between Americo-Liberians and the republic's ethnic peoples created a situation that eventually exploded into war.

In 1980 Samuel K. Doe, a Liberian soldier from the Krahn ethnic group, led the violent overthrow of the Americo-Liberian government. Doe headed the new military government and became the first person from an African ethnic group to rule Liberia. At first many people were in favor of Doe, who promised to give more opportunities to Liberia's ethnic peoples. But Doe did not allow free speech, and for several years he banned political organizations. Journalists, politicians, and other people who spoke out against Doe were sent to prison or executed. Doe became more and more unpopular, and various leaders tried to overthrow his government during the 1980s.

Samuel Doe makes a speech in 1980, the year he overthrew the government of Liberia.

Charles Taylor, head of the rebel National Patriotic Front of Liberia (NPFL), answers reporters' questions during a public appearance in 1990.

In December 1989, an Americo-Liberian named Charles Taylor gathered support among the Gio and the Mano peoples. He formed an army called the National Patriotic Front of Liberia (NPFL). Hoping to overthrow Doe, the NPFL advanced against Doe's army, the Armed Forces of Liberia (AFL). In return AFL soldiers murdered and raped Gio, Mano, and other innocent citizens, while the NPFL attacked soldiers and innocent people in Krahn areas. Francis, who is Mano, says, "Doe started killing my people and that started the war."

By July 1990, the NPFL had entered Monrovia. The AFL, the NPFL, and the Independent National Patriotic Front of Liberia (INPFL)—a group that had split from the NPFL—fought for control of the capital city. Many innocent Liberians were killed or driven from their homes. Francis remembers that because he was Mano, "So many times [the AFL soldiers] came to my house looking for me."

An organization called the Economic Community of West African States (ECOWAS) soon began working with Liberia's warring armies to try to bring peace. In August 1990, ECOWAS sent peacekeeping forces to Monrovia. After the INPFL killed Doe in September,

Fighting among Liberia's rebel factions continued in 1996, engaging eager youths, who saw little future for themselves outside of the nation's longstanding war.

ECOWAS helped name a new Liberian president. Since 1990 ECOWAS and other groups have negotiated countless peace agreements in Liberia. But new enemy groups have formed, and the brutal ethnic fighting continues. No one knows how or when the war will come to an end.

NPFL rebel troops flee gunfire in the outskirts of Monrovia. By 1990 fighting around the city had made it virtually impossible for residents to lead normal lives.

During the fighting in Monrovia in 1990, Liberians faced shortages of food, medicine, and other daily necessities. From time to time, the Millers went out into the city in search of food. But traveling through Monrovia was dangerous. Armed soldiers from all factions (groups) roamed the streets. Francis remembers that soldiers were suspicious of everyone. To avoid being shot, "You had to really explain yourself," Francis recalls.

Maryetta adds, "If you were Mano or Mandingo, they would kill you. That was why I was so happy that they didn't kill Francis. I was afraid for him because he is Mano."

One day Gondah, the oldest Miller son, went into the city to look for food. He did not return and hasn't been seen or heard from since.

The Millers' youngest daughter, Yah, was one year old at this time. When she became sick, Pearl and Francis could not get to a hospital or doctor to find out what was wrong with her. With no medicine and already weak from lack of food, Yah died.

Francis has never forgotten his daughter's death. "We were looking at her. She was in our hands when she took her last breath. There was nothing we could do."

Kau (center), *her mother, Pearl* (left), *and a family friend* (right) *relax in the family's kitchen in Houston. In Liberia Pearl had to decide whether to lead her children on the dangerous journey out of Monrovia or to remain in the city, where life became more uncertain every day.*

As time passed, food became even more scarce. Francis headed to the countryside in search of food for his family. While he was gone, the fighting in Monrovia worsened. Pearl was frightened for her family's safety. So she chose to flee the city with her children.

Leaving Monrovia was a difficult decision for Pearl. She had no idea where Francis was or how to reach him. But Pearl knew that if she wanted to protect her family, she had to get out of the city quickly.

Many residents of Monrovia were heading toward the city's port to board boats bound for Ghana, a country to the east of Côte d'Ivoire. But some of the heaviest fighting in the city was in the port district. And Pearl had also heard stories about frantic pushing and shoving as large crowds fought for space on the boats.

Pearl knew that she would have trouble managing alone in a crowd with her five young children. So she traveled northward out of town instead of going to the port. Charles Taylor's soldiers controlled this northern area of Liberia, so the family would not have to face active fighting there.

Pearl and her children fled Monrovia on foot. The only possessions they took with them were the clothes on their backs. They heard gunfire and explosions all around. Buildings and cars were on fire. Looters went through homes and businesses, taking whatever they wanted. Somehow the Millers managed to pass

By the time the Millers fled Monrovia, much of the city was reduced to deserted streets marked by trash, vandalized cars and buildings, and an occasional rebel soldier.

through the city unharmed. After they got outside the city, the Millers joined a slow, steady stream of refugees walking across the countryside. It seemed as if everyone was abandoning Monrovia.

The Millers and the other refugees traveled along a road that led to the Liberian district of Fendell. Before the war, Fendell had a university. But when heavy fighting began in Monrovia, Fendell became a vast refugee encampment. Tens of thousands of refugees slept wherever they could in the area.

Liberian refugees gather at a refugee camp in Fendell, an outer district of Monrovia.

In normal times, the walk to Fendell might have taken 10 or 12 hours. But in wartime, the trip took much longer. Soldiers at the many checkpoints along the way stopped everyone. They took food and valuables and questioned people to see if they were enemy soldiers. Many of the soldiers at the checkpoints were young boys. The AK-47 automatic rifles they carried could fire as many as 30 bullets with one pull of the trigger.

Nya has a distant look on his face when he recalls the danger his family faced at each checkpoint. "You didn't say anything until [the soldiers] asked you. You did what they told you." The Millers witnessed numerous killings at the checkpoints. Some of the victims were people the family had met along the way.

Every day Pearl and her children wondered if they would ever see Francis again. They knew he might disappear like Gondah and so many others had. And the family was still mourning the loss of baby Yah.

Meanwhile Francis had joined the flow of refugees heading north out of Monrovia. He didn't know that Pearl and the children had also left.

Francis describes passing through the checkpoints. "Ten, twelve year olds holding guns. They were the most dangerous ones, the most feared. The first thing they would ask you was your tribe. They asked you so many questions. They searched you for weapons. That was not an easy process."

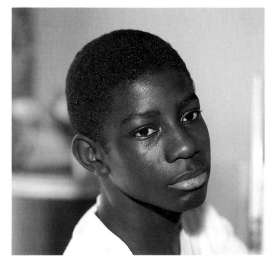

Nya was only 10 years old when his family fled to the refugee camp in Fendell.

 Pearl knew people who had fled Monrovia earlier and who were staying with friends in Fendell. These friends offered Pearl and the children shelter.

One of Francis's brothers, Augustus, had also fled to Fendell from Monrovia. One day Uncle Augustus went to a gate in Fendell through which most refugees passed to enter the city. He stood at the gate watching, hoping to see his brother. That afternoon he was rewarded to see a tired Francis Miller walking into Fendell. The two men were so happy to see each other! They hugged and shook hands.

Uncle Augustus took Francis to Pearl and the children. They all hugged Francis and screamed with happiness.

After they were reunited, the Miller family left Fendell and continued their journey. Because they wanted to get as far away from the fighting as possible, the family traveled deeper into the interior of Liberia to the town of Kakata.

The Millers were fortunate. The commander of Charles Taylor's army had a pickup truck that he used to move people out of the overcrowded camp at Fendell. By truck the journey to Kakata took only an hour.

Traveling across the hilly terrain on foot would have taken several days.

Francis says, "[The driver was] very nice. He was helping people. We were just lucky. We were at the gate that morning, and he took us to Kakata."

The Millers stayed in Kakata for several months, hoping that the fighting would end and they could return to Monrovia. But the fighting continued. So Francis and Pearl decided to go to Côte d'Ivoire. Francis had heard that from there, employees of the U.S. government could get to the United States. Since Francis had worked for the Voice of America radio station, he thought he and his family might have a chance.

Francis borrowed money to travel by bus ahead of his family to Danané, Côte d'Ivoire. The journey took two days. From Côte d'Ivoire, Francis turned to the U.S. Embassy for help. The embassy was able to contact the Voice of America, which forwarded Francis's back pay. Francis used this money to buy bus tickets to Danané for Pearl and the children.

Like all Liberian refugees in the city, the Millers had to register with the United Nations, an international organization, to receive a small monthly food ration, which included milk, rice, cornmeal, and sugar. The family stayed temporarily with a friend of Francis's, and the Miller children went to a school set up by Liberian refugees. Meanwhile, Francis looked for work.

Before leaving Monrovia, Francis worked for the Voice of America, a radio station run by the United States Information Agency.

He says, "If you didn't have money, you couldn't make it. The soldiers took everything from you along the way. How was a poor refugee going to get money to pay for things? I will never, ever forget those days in Ivory Coast. You had nothing to do. You sat and wondered, What will I do today? What will I do so my children can eat?"

Francis supported his family with his back pay and by doing odd jobs. For most of the time in Côte d'Ivoire, he handled a push-push cart loaded with goods to sell. "It was a big cart and when it was loaded, it was heavy!" Francis recalls.

In time Francis found a house to rent near Danané. After the Millers had been in Côte d'Ivoire for a few months, they learned that one of Francis's sisters, Cynthia, and her family had escaped to Ghana. Francis traveled there to see her.

"When I reached Ghana, it was easy. Nobody asked you a thing. When you said you were from Liberia, they knew you had problems," Francis remembers.

But everything in Ghana cost more than it did in Côte d'Ivoire. And Francis and Pearl wanted a permanent, safe home for their family. They wanted to begin a new life. So Francis returned to Danané, where he began a long series of interviews with U.S. immigration officials. The family was eventually approved for immigration because Francis had worked for the U.S.

Francis was determined to find a safe place for his family to live.

government. After being approved, the family had to see doctors. All the Millers were tested for a variety of diseases, including AIDS. Anyone with these diseases was refused permission to immigrate to the United States. The Millers passed the tests.

 Pearl's mother, Maryetta, had lived just outside Monrovia for most of her life. In 1990 Maryetta's husband, Robert, was taken away by rebel soldiers. Robert was from the Vai tribe. But the soldiers were certain that he was Mandingo, so they killed him.

For safety Maryetta decided to join Pearl and Francis in Monrovia. She recalls her farewell to her neighbors. "I said, 'Let us pray.' We knelt down in my house, and we had a word of prayer. Then we got up, and I started going."

But Maryetta had no idea Pearl had already fled Monrovia. When she arrived at Pearl's home, she found no sign of her daughter's family. Maryetta discovered that the Millers' home had been looted. Whatever people had not carried away was scattered about in the yard and on the street. Maryetta searched through the remains. She found little of value except for two photos of Yah, which she put in her pocket.

After rebel fighters killed her husband, Maryetta King left her home and eventually fled Liberia. Now living in Houston, she prays for the safety of family members remaining in the war-torn country and hopes one day to return home.

The Miller family took off from Abidjan, Côte d'Ivoire, on their journey to the United States.

Maryetta then went to stay with other family members in Monrovia. They eventually learned that the Millers had reached Côte d'Ivoire safely. Not long afterward, Maryetta left Monrovia and joined Pearl and her family in Danané.

In September 1992, Francis, Pearl, and their children left Côte d'Ivoire for the United States. Maryetta remained behind, waiting for official approval to immigrate to the United States, where she later joined her family. A private refugee agency called the International Organization for Migration (IOM), which works with the U.S. government, handled the paperwork and made travel arrangements for the Millers. The IOM also contacted Refugee Services Alliance (RSA), which agreed to help the Millers get settled in the United States.

The Miller family flew first from Abidjan, Côte d'Ivoire, to Brussels, Belgium, in Europe. In Brussels the family transferred to a flight to New York City. RSA staff members met the Millers at the airport in New York and helped the family fill out immigration papers. Then the family boarded a plane for their new home in Houston, Texas.

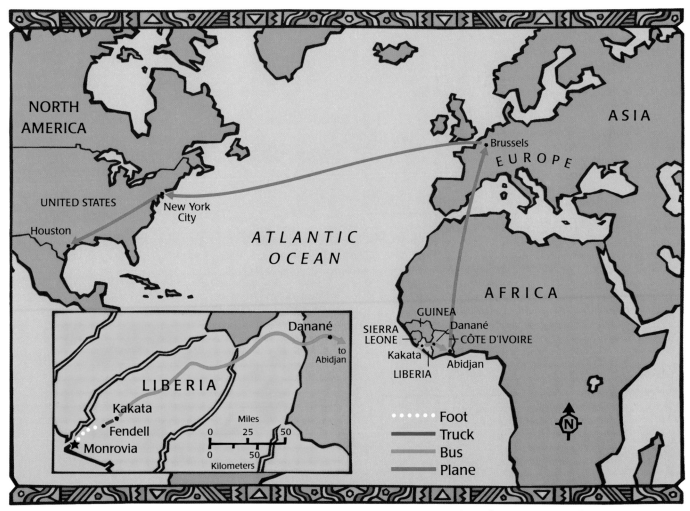

The Millers flew from Côte d'Ivoire to New York City, stopping over briefly in Europe. Once in the United States, the Millers continued on from New York to Houston, Texas.

(From left to right) *Thomas, Maryetta, Augustus, and Kau take a stroll near downtown Houston.*

The Millers didn't exactly choose Houston. The IOM in Danané had asked Francis where he wanted to live in the United States. At that time, Francis didn't know much about the United States. He did know that the weather could be very cold in some parts of the country. So he told the IOM that he wanted to live where it wasn't cold. The IOM chose Houston, Texas.

RSA representatives met the Millers at the airport in Houston. They took the Millers to the family's new home in an apartment complex in northeastern Houston.

Other Miller family members also live in the United States. Francis's brother Thomas lived in New Jersey before moving in with Francis and his family in Houston. Their sister Cynthia lives in Philadelphia, Pennsylvania. Two other sisters, Ellen and Ivy, live in Rhode Island. Francis comments, "The war caused us to scatter all around."

Maryetta is thankful. She says, "If we did not have the Lord, we would not be here. He took us to a lot of places."

Not long after moving in, Francis bought a basketball, a football, and a soccer ball for his family. The equipment didn't last long. Augustus shakes his head. "We left them on the patio, and they took everything." The Millers don't know who stole the athletic equipment. Such things didn't happen in their old neighborhood in Monrovia, where people watched out for one another.

Augustus plays soccer for his high-school team in Houston.

Kau enjoys a snack.

Francis compares life in Liberia to life in the United States. "In Liberia we had a kind of communal life. Everyone cared about the welfare of others. I hardly know anyone [in the United States]. In Liberia I knew almost everyone, even my neighbor's children. There I could discipline other children, just as I discipline my own children. No one would be angry. [The child's] mother and father would congratulate me for that. If you would yell 'Rogue!' everyone would come and grab the [offender]. That is how the community was brought up. That was the kind of communal life we lived. It is not like that here."

After awhile the Millers moved into a three-bedroom apartment in a giant apartment complex in the southwestern part of the city. Many people who live in the complex are from different parts of the world, including Mexico, Central America, and Africa. The Beltway, a multilane superhighway, can be seen from the Millers' landing, which leads to their second-floor apartment.

Although the Millers' new apartment is bigger than the previous one, the family remains cramped in their space. They hope to have a bigger home one day, with enough room to fit everyone comfortably.

The family is cramped in their new home. Each bedroom is crammed with beds, and at night Uncle Thomas sleeps on the foldout sofa in the living room. Security is a big concern for the Millers, too. The electronic gates at the entrance and exit to the apartment complex are often stuck open. A sheriff's deputy, who lives in the complex, provides some sense of security when he's home. But the deputy can't prevent all the car thefts, violence, and other crimes that occur in the neighborhood.

(Right, from left to right) *Augustus, Deazee, and Nya clown around together. Although it took them awhile to make new friends, the Miller children have adjusted well to life in Houston.* (Below) *Kau (left) and a friend goof off outside the Millers' apartment. Kau is eating a slice of Liberian rice bread.*

At first the Miller children had problems being accepted in their new country. Francis was very concerned. He remembers, "There was always fighting on the school bus and in the neighborhood."

Nya explains, "It was because we spoke differently and acted differently." The boys stood their ground, and Nya emphasizes that they no longer have problems. "My friends don't care where I'm from. I've got friends of every color. I don't care where they're from."

Francis and Pearl face their own challenges. They haven't been able to find jobs that they like and that pay well. For the time being, they have demanding jobs, where they work long hours for low wages. Francis describes the situation. "Right now America is a little frustrating for us. We barely meet our expenses."

Although Francis and Pearl worry about making ends meet, they still believe they made the right choice in coming to the United States.

Thomas watches television at home.

Francis works nights at a hospital. By the time he gets home after midnight, everyone is asleep. He doesn't see his wife or children much during the week. Intelligent and educated, Francis has had a hard time accepting his job. Yet he's willing to do whatever it takes to support his family.

In the evening, Francis often calls his children from work. Like many parents, he worries that his children watch too much television. There is little to do at the apartment complex, which doesn't have a playground or any nearby parks. So the children turn to television for entertainment.

"I always tell them to read if they don't have anything to do. I tell them to read something because reading is very important," Francis says. Nya adds, "Our teachers also encourage us to read." The Miller children do enjoy reading. Nya liked the autobiography of Malcolm X, a civil rights leader. He is also a fan of short stories by O. Henry. Augustus's favorite book is *To Kill a Mockingbird* by Harper Lee.

When the Millers first arrived in Houston, Pearl worked as a cashier in a convenience store and went to school to earn a certificate as a nurse's aid. With her certificate, Pearl was able to find a job at a senior citizens' home. She works from early in the morning until the middle of the afternoon, including weekends.

Augustus follows the news by reading the daily newspaper.

Like his wife, Francis recognizes the importance of education. He is taking classes at a community college in Houston so he can become a radiology technician at the hospital. He goes to school on Saturdays and Sundays, which takes up the little free time he once had with his children.

Maryetta wants to help Pearl and Francis support the family, too. For a time, she worked for an elderly person in his home. But when the man became too ill to live at home, Maryetta lost her job. She continues to search for work and welcomes her grandchildren home from school each afternoon. But she says, "It's so hard to sit here all day."

Francis speaks for his family when he says he feels they were misled about what life would be like in the United States. "We thought America was a glory land—like milk and honey. Our own people didn't tell us what America was like!"

Augustus, Nya, Thomas, Kau, and Deazee all like the United States very much and want to be considered Americans. But they agree with their father when they say that the United States is not at all what any of

(Above) *Kau and Augustus ponder the view from the dining room window of their Houston apartment.*
(Left, from left to right) *Deazee, Thomas, and Augustus decorate the family's Christmas tree. The Millers are Christians and belong to the United Methodist Church.*

them expected before they arrived. What did they expect? All of the Miller kids chime in at the same time. "That it would be fun and easy!" What is the reality? "There's nothing to do. We can't even get summer jobs," they say.

 Religion has always been an important part of the Millers' life, and the family attends church services regularly in the United States. It has been through their church in Houston that the Millers have been able to establish some sense of community in their new home.

As a boy growing up in Liberia, Francis attended a Methodist school run by Christian missionaries who were in Liberia to teach their religion to local Africans. In Houston Francis and his family attend Gethsemane United Methodist Church, which is run by the Reverend Dr. Charles Greene. Dr. Greene is proud that he has 14 refugee families from West Africa among his congregation.

Kau hurries to catch up with her family after church.

Augustus (left), *Maryetta* (right center), *and Francis* (right) *chat with the Reverend Greene* (left center), *the minister at Gethsemane United Methodist Church.*

Maryetta says, "I don't like to live anywhere without the church. The first time I visited [Gethsemane], I liked it. The people are very friendly. I love Reverend Greene's preaching. He preaches well." She adds that in Liberia, her sister married a man whose last name was Greene. She laughs and says, "I told [the Reverend Greene] that maybe we are related."

The Miller children have made connections through their schools as well as through their church. Each one of the Miller children rides a different school bus to a different school in the city. Deazee, who is in third grade, and Kau, who is in fifth grade, went to the same elementary school for one year. But because the school became overcrowded, Kau goes to another school.

Kau gets up every morning at 6:30 A.M. She has to be in front of the apartment complex before 7:10 A.M. to catch the school bus. Some of her brothers get up even earlier.

School in the United States is much different than it was in Liberia. Nya explains, "We have better facilities here. Sometimes we have movies in the classrooms on geography and other subjects. We switch classes here. We didn't there. We spent all day in the same classroom. We had no computers there and no televisions."

From time to time, teachers take a special interest in the Miller children. For example, one teacher used to take Nya and Augustus to chess tournaments on weekends. The two boys were competitive. Nya smiles and admits, "Every time Augustus beat me, I would mess up the board!"

One of Kau's art teachers occasionally drops by the Millers' home to check on her. Like her brothers, Kau has a talent for art. Her favorite subjects to draw are dogs and flowers. A poster she drew won third place in a contest at school and was displayed at a local store.

Kau (in striped shirt) and her classmates board the school bus early in the morning.

THE VINGANANEE AND THE TREE TOAD

Long before the civil war in Liberia, old men gathered in the villages of the interior to tell stories about their community. In the mid-1900s, villagers began leaving their tribal homes to find jobs in Monrovia. Many children growing up in Monrovia never had an opportunity to attend a gathering of elders because the young people lived so far from their family's ancestral villages. So in the 1950s, an Americo-Liberian named Clara Blaine-Wilson started a radio show called the Kiddies' Korner Program to tell Liberian folktales to the people of Monrovia. This is one of the stories she told.

A long time ago, Spider bought a big farm and hired Lion and Buck Deer to work the fields for him. He hired Rat to cook and clean. The animals lived together in Spider's house. Every day Lion and Buck Deer worked in the fields. At night they came home to eat the stew that Rat had cooked. When they went to bed, Tree Toad sang them all to sleep.

One day while Rat was sweeping the floor, he heard someone coming. Rat looked out the door and saw a strange, bushy animal heading toward the house singing, "I'm the Vingananee, and I am hungry. Give me your stew, or I will eat you!" Rat ran out and hit the Vingananee with his broom. The two got into a fight, which the Vingananee won. He dragged Rat behind the house and tied him up. Then he ate up all the stew.

When Spider, Buck Deer, and Lion came home, they saw Rat tied up and asked him what had happened. After Rat told them, Buck Deer said, "I'm big. I'm tough. Tomorrow I will stay home and if that Vingananee comes, I'll kick him." Everyone felt better. They cooked and ate their dinner. Then they went to bed, and Tree Toad sang them all to sleep.

The next day, while Buck Deer was sweeping, he heard the Vingananee singing the same song he'd sung the day before. Buck Deer asked the creature what he wanted. When the Vingananee said he wanted to eat the stew, Buck Deer hit him with the broom. The two got into a fight, which the Vingananee won. He dragged Buck Deer behind the house and tied him up. Then he ate up all the stew.

When Spider, Lion, and Rat came home, they found Buck Deer tied up. When he told them about the Vingananee, Lion roared, "I'm the king of the animals. I'll stay home tomorrow, and if the Vingananee comes, I will kill him!" Everyone felt better. They cooked and ate their dinner. Then they went to bed, and Tree Toad sang them to sleep.

The next day, the same thing happened. When Lion tried to stop the Vingananee, the creature dragged him behind the house and tied him up. Then he ate up all the stew.

When Spider and his friends came home, they couldn't believe their eyes. They found Lion tied up and no stew in the pot. This time Tree Toad volunteered to stay home the next day. The other animals laughed because Tree Toad was so small. "How can you fight the Vingananee?" they said. "I can try," replied Tree Toad.

The animals untied Lion. They cooked and ate their dinner. Then they went to bed, and Tree Toad sang them to sleep. The next morning, the animals said good-bye to Tree Toad. They were sure they would never see her again. "We will miss your song," they said.

Tree Toad made the stew. As she was sweeping the floor, she heard someone coming. Sure enough, down the path came the Vingananee. He was singing, "I'm the Vingananee, and I am hungry. Give me your stew, or I will eat you!"

Tree Toad took the broom to stop the Vingananee, but the creature grabbed Tree Toad and threw her into the air four times. Tree Toad couldn't stand it. She looked up at the sky and said, "God, I can't fight the Vingananee. You must help me." The next time the Vingananee threw Tree Toad into the air, she landed on the creature's head. The Vingananee fell over and lay quiet. Tree Toad got some rope, tied up the Vingananee, and sat down to wait.

When the others came home, they were sad. They expected to find Tree Toad dead. But instead they found the Vingananee tied up and Tree Toad sitting right beside him. Spider asked, "Tree Toad, how did you fight the Vingananee and win?" "It was a miracle!" cried Tree Toad.

This story is adapted from The Vingananee and the Tree Toad, *retold by Verna Aardema (Viking Kestrel, 1988).*

 On Saturday, while Pearl and Francis are at work and at school, Maryetta and her grandchildren visit the Houston Zoo. At the zoo, the family see a lot of things that remind them of Liberia. They watch monkeys, chimpanzees, antelope, and hippopotamuses. They also join the crowds watching the elephants.

But of all the animals at the zoo, the most exciting for the Millers are in the reptile house. Deazee especially wants to see the snakes. His older brothers and sister lead the way. At one of the windows in the reptile house, Kau and Thomas both recognize a Gaboon viper. This deadly snake is native to West Africa. Kau and Thomas shout, "We've seen those before in Liberia! You would see them anywhere. You had to look out for them!" Augustus looks at the snake and nods. "I killed this kind of snake one time."

At a rain-forest exhibit, Nya comments, "They taught us in school about the importance of the rain forest. They contain many important plants that may help scientists cure diseases such as AIDS."

Maryetta and her grandchildren enjoy a day at the Houston Zoo.

(Right, from left to right) *Deazee, Augustus, and Thomas stroll through a park in Houston.* (Above) *Nya sometimes likes to keep to himself.*

The Millers love sports. In Liberia Augustus and Nya played soccer. Augustus plays soccer for his high school in Houston. But in the United States, Nya prefers basketball. Thomas, Kau, and Deazee all agree with Nya. And like many young boys, Thomas and Deazee dream of playing for the National Basketball Association some day. Francis tries to discourage such talk. He wants his children to focus on their education.

The Millers' apartment complex once had a basketball hoop at the edge of the parking lot. But someone broke the rim off the rusting backboard, and the hoop has never been replaced. Deazee and his friends found an abandoned metal grocery cart, which they used as their basket for awhile. Then someone removed the cart.

Most people in Houston know of Hakeem Olajuwon of the Houston Rockets' basketball team. Olajuwon, who is originally from the West African country of Nigeria, means a great deal to young African immigrants like the Miller children. They admire him as an African who has been very successful in the United States. All the Miller children are now big fans of the Houston Rockets.

Michael Jordan, a basketball star who plays for the Chicago Bulls, also holds a special place in the Millers' hearts. Thomas especially is a big fan and has read Jordan's biography. A poster of the basketball star hangs in the room he shares with his brothers.

Thomas chomps on a lollipop as he takes a shot at an imaginary basketball hoop, because the apartment complex no longer has a hoop.

Maryetta and Augustus prepare most of the family meals. Augustus does much of the cooking himself, and everyone agrees that he is a great cook. Kau says she helps, but Augustus is quick to say she doesn't. He grins and adds, "She knows Hamburger Helper."

The Miller family generally eat Liberian food. A typical meal, for example, consists of rice with greens (leafy plants cooked as vegetables). Maryetta smiles and says, "We love our rice!"

Rice can be expensive in Liberia. Many people substitute a starchy root vegetable called cassava. Cassavas are something like potatoes. To prepare cassava, cooks peel the roots of the plant and boil them until they are soft. Then they pound the cassava into a pulp using a large mortar (bowl) and pestle (a small utensil for pounding or grinding).

To make a popular West African dish called *fufu*, Liberian cooks add water to the cassava pulp and shape the mixture into round dumplings. Then they cover the dumplings with spicy greens, meat, or fish stew. West Africans like spicy food. Augustus warns guests, "Liberians use very hot peppers. I mean so hot that you can even cry!"

Ground-up cassava is available in Houston, but it is quite expensive. So Augustus mixes a small amount of flaked tapioca (a processed form of cassava) with large

Augustus stirs up a batch of fufu, *a traditional West African food. With his parents working long hours, Augustus often cooks for the family.*

Kau prepares some sandwiches for an after-school snack.

quantities of instant mashed potato flakes. He cooks the mixture in the microwave. The result is a lot like the cassava the family ate in Liberia. A large, covered mixing bowl filled with newly made fufu is often on the counter at the Miller home, while fish stew simmers in a large pot on top of the stove. Augustus says, "We eat fufu because it is the food of our home[land]."

Because Kau and Deazee were so young when they left Liberia, they don't remember much about Liberian food. They prefer hamburgers and pizza. But fast food is a treat that the Millers don't have very often because it's too expensive for the family's budget. Even though the family has limited money for food, they think of this as a minor problem in comparison to the hunger and danger they experienced in Liberia.

 Francis and Pearl want their children to have a sense of their Liberian heritage. They wish their children knew more about the traditions and cultures of their ancestors. Pearl's father, for example, was from the Vai people. Her grandfather was Bassa. Francis is proud of his Mano heritage.

Augustus thinks about his own heritage as he examines a library display on black history.

But the Miller children were all born and raised in Monrovia, where people from Liberia's many different tribal groups live and blend their cultures. The children speak English, and what little of their father's Mano language they once knew, they have forgotten since they fled Liberia. Kau and Nya do have Mano tribal names. Kau's name means "first-born daughter." Nya's name means "second-born son."

The Miller children appreciate their heritage, but they are focused on being part of American culture. As one of the older children, Augustus remembers Liberia best. One day he pauses to look at an exhibit for Black History Month in the window of a Houston library. The exhibit shows many colorful masks from different parts of Africa. Augustus thinks about Liberian masks as he looks at the exhibit. He comments, "The war destroyed everything in Liberia."

Houston's yearly International Festival is a major event that attracts thousands of people every spring to downtown Houston. Six stages feature performers from around the world. This spring the festival honors the countries of West Africa.

At first the Miller children aren't sure if they are interested in going to the festival. Francis thinks he might not be able to attend because of school. But late one afternoon, Francis returns home and rounds up everyone for the event. His enthusiasm is contagious.

When they arrive at the festival, the Millers are surprised to see how big it is. Thousands of people are milling about. Famous performers from West Africa ignite the crowd. Everywhere people dance to the beat of the music.

The festival attracts West Africans from all over Houston. Francis runs into many friends he hasn't seen for some time. Some are Liberians who, like the Millers, have resettled in Houston. While their father mingles with West African friends, the Miller children listen to the music from the main stage. Then they head to the nearby exhibit called the African Village.

(Above, from left to right) *Deazee, Thomas, and Kau share a laugh at the Houston International Festival.* (Left) *Crowds listen to a West African musical group at the festival.*

(Below) *Deazee explores the festival's African Village.* (Right) *Thomas takes a seat in a royal throne from Ghana in the African Village.*

Each structure in the village represents a different West African country. At each stop, visitors can get a glimpse of a traditional West African culture, such as a performance and ritual area from Nigeria and a medicine hut from Gambia. The Millers also see a market-place from Togo and a kitchen from Senegal. They see a Palava Hut from Liberia, too. The Millers know that in the interior of Liberia, village elders gather at such a hut to listen to arguments from opposing sides and then make a judgment. Francis explains, "When a Liberian says, 'We have a Palava,' it means we have certain differences we must settle."

Later the Millers wander through the open-air market and the booths that sell West African food. The Millers choose pizza, turkey legs, and tacos instead. They have West African food at home every day!

In the years before the war, Monrovia had many festivals. Francis smiles as he remembers. "The Christmas holidays were a sight to see. Monrovia would be so crowded!" July 26—Liberian Independence Day—was another major holiday. Parades featured marching bands and drill teams. Augustus remembers best the festivals with "many people in native dress, African music, the beating of drums." Most striking were masked and costumed performers from the Poro (a secret society), who danced in continuous spins. "There were many dance competitions," Augustus adds. "They were very exciting."

Kau and her father enjoy a bite to eat.

59

At about the same time as the Houston International Festival, the Millers host their own celebration at home. Pearl and Francis each have a birthday this week. The family invites close friends to a small party at their apartment. People dance to West African music playing on the stereo, and the Liberian guests sing along to the familiar songs.

The birthday food is spicy hot. Guests enjoy flavored greens and barbecued beef, West African style. A sweet bread made of rice, bananas, and molasses is a pleasant surprise. For a time, the Liberian refugees can pretend they are back home.

At the birthday party for Francis and Pearl, Francis (above) *samples a spicy Liberian dish. Later, Pearl and some of her guests* (right) *pose together for a group photo.*

The Millers keep their memories in a small photo album. In the front are the two photos of Yah that Maryetta picked up from the Millers' yard in Monrovia. There are also photos of family events and friends. Maryetta wants to send some of the photos to relatives in Liberia. But the children want to keep the photos. For the time being, the photos stay in the album.

Although the Millers' life in the United States is not always easy, they accept the challenges. They are rebuilding their lives in Houston, and it's unlikely they will return to Liberia, where civil war continues to rage.

Maryetta has a different view. She wants very much to return to her mother, her sisters, and the nieces and nephews who remain in Liberia. She wishes that all of the family could live in one place. She says, "When the war ends, I will go home by the grace of God."

As with many refugee families, the Millers' life in the United States is bittersweet. The family appreciate the freedoms they have in America, but they miss their relatives. The Millers also wonder if they will ever achieve the comfortable standard of living they once had in their homeland. They realize that their former world has disappeared and that they must work hard to make a good life in their new home. Francis and Pearl have great hope and faith that things will work out, especially for their children, who represent the family's future in America.

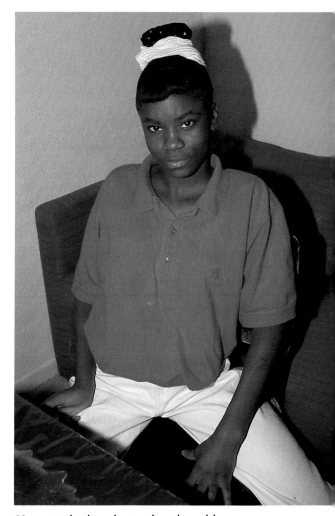

Kau works hard at school and hopes for a bright and promising future.

FURTHER READING

Aardema, Verna. *The Vingananee and the Tree Toad: A Liberian Tale.* New York: Viking Kestrel, 1988.

Aardema, Verna. *Why Mosquitoes Buzz in People's Ears: A West African Tale.* New York: Dial Books for Young Readers, 1975.

Bess, Clayton. *Story for a Black Night.* Boston: Houghton Mifflin, 1982.

Davis, Russell, and Brent Ashabranner. *Land in the Sun: The Story of West Africa.* Boston: Little, Brown, 1963.

Ellis, Veronica Freeman. *Land of the Four Winds.* Orange, New Jersey: Just Us Books, 1993.

Humphrey, Sally. *A Family in Liberia.* Minneapolis: Lerner Publications Company, 1987.

Liberia in Pictures. Minneapolis: Lerner Publications Company, 1988.

Stewart, Gail B. *Liberia.* New York: Crestwood House, 1992.

PRONUNCIATION GUIDE

Abidjan (ab-ih-JAHN)
Bassa (BAH-suh)
Côte d'Ivoire (KOHT deev-WAHR)
Danané (DAH-nah-nay)
Deazee (dee-AH-zee)
Gethsemane (gehth-SEH-muh-nee)
Ghana (GAHN-uh)
Gio (GEE-oh)
Gondah (guhn-DAH)
Guinea (GIHN-ee)
Kakata (KAH-kah-tah)
Kau (KOW)
Liberia (ly-BIHR-ee-uh)
Mano (MAH-noh)
Maryetta (mah-ree-EH-tuh)
Monrovia (muhn-ROH-vee-uh)
Nigeria (ny-JIHR-ee-uh)
Nya (NYAH)
Olajuwon, Hakeem (oh-LAH-juh-wahn, ah-KEEM)
Sierra Leone (see-EHR-uh lee-OHN)

INDEX

ABOUT THE AUTHOR

Stephen Chicoine was born and raised in Decatur, Illinois. A graduate of the University of Illinois and of Stanford University, he has traveled extensively throughout the world. Mr. Chicoine has also written *Journey Between Two Worlds: A Tibetan Family* and has coauthored a book for young adults about Lithuania. He is currently at work on several other books for children and young adults. Mr. Chicoine makes his home in Houston, Texas, with his wife and family.

PHOTO ACKNOWLEDGMENTS

Cover photos by Reuters/Chadi Matar/Archive Photos (left) and Stephen Chicoine (right). All inside photos by Stephen Chicoine except the following: © Liba Taylor/Panos Pictures, pp. 6, 7, 8, 9; The Hutchison Library, pp. 13, 28; Schomburg Center for Research in Black Culture, New York Public Library, p. 17; The Bettmann Archive, p. 18; © Maurice Harvey/The Hutchison Library, p. 34; Reuters/Frederick Neema/Archive Photos, p. 15; National Archives/Photo # 83-FB-272, p. 16; Library of Congress, p. 19 (left); Archive Photos, p. 20; UPI/Corbis-Bettmann, p. 21; Reuters/Corbis-Bettmann, p. 22; Reuters/Corinne Dufka/Archive Photos, p. 23; Reuters/Archive Photos, p. 24; © Martin Adler/Panos Pictures, p. 27; Voice of America, p. 31. Cut-ins: Details from a Liberian fabric reproduced with permission from the Trustees of the British Museum. All artwork and maps by Laura Westlund.